Stay young with Qi Gong!

Volume 6: Bone Marrow-Qi Gong and Embryonic breathing

Qi Gong is part of Traditional Chinese Medicine (TCM) and is practiced by millions of people around the world today. The goal is to maintain body and mind health and thus lead a long, happy life. This is done with a combination of traditional movements, breathing methods and the power of imagination. Everyone can start learning Qi Gong regardless of age, previous knowledge or constitution - ideally today!

The author has been teaching Kung Fu and Qi Gong at his own school for many years. He had previously learned both arts from European and Chinese masters. His Qi Gong books contain useful knowledge and practical instructions in a compact, easy-to-understand form. Jin means "today" and Dao means "the way".

Stay young with Qi Gong!, Volume 6
1st edition, February 2023
Copyright © Jin Dao 2023
Cover image: pixabay.com
Photos: Marlon
Production and Publishing: BoD - Books on Demand, Norderstedt
ISBN: 978-3741281013

JIN DAO-Publishing
66424 Homburg, Germany
www.WT-Saarpfalz.de
E-Mail: Kontakt@WT-Saarpfalz.de

CONTENT

INTRODUCTION 3
GENERAL PART 5
The Three Treasures 5
   Jing 7
   Qi 8
   Shen 9
   The relationship between the Three Treasures 10
How can we avoid diseases? 11
Feng Shui 12
Qi and plants 14
Mindfulness 15
How do I know that my Qi Gong training is successful? 16
PRACTICAL PART 18
Bone Marrow-Qi Gong 18
   The importance of the exercises 18
   Bone breathing 21
   Bone compression 26
   Bone marrow washing 32
   Summary of the exercises 37
   Final exercises 41
Embryonic breathing 47
   The goals of Embryonic breathing 47
   The practice of Embryonic breathing 48
   Summary of the Embryonic breathing 50
OVERVIEW OF THE PRACTICAL CONTENT OF THE SERIES 52

Introduction

This book is part of a series in which I try to share my experience in Qi Gong with interested people and enable them to start practicing on their own. I have always based myself on the following structure:

General part - practical part.

The general part includes some basic knowledge that is important for understanding Qi Gong. I concentrated on the essentials and tried to use an understandable expression.

The practical part only contains exercise instructions that I have been practicing successfully for a long time and which I teach in my Qi Gong school. Furthermore, all exercises are suitable for self-study and can be done safely if carried out conscientiously. Of course, the example of a real teacher and practicing in a group where a common energy circle is formed can never be completely replaced.
The instructions given in the volumes in this series are sufficient material for every need and for lifelong practice.

If, in individual cases, any health risks should be expected due to the individual constitution of the practitioner, it is recommended to consult a doctor.

As far as the rendering of Chinese expressions is concerned, I have not opted for a single method of Romanization (e.g. Yale, Wade-Giles), but always for the commonly used and known form.

Someone who has started Qi Gong training will in most cases not want to stop any more. Once you have felt the pleasant feeling of the flow of energy and learned the ability to control your own Qi, not only will you be very satisfied, but our whole life will be positively influenced by it.

A quote from Laozi, the founder of Daoism, from the 6th century BC, reads:

"Even a journey of a thousand miles begins with the first step."

General part

The Three Treasures

In Chinese philosophy, body and mind are merely viewed as different manifestations of Qi. The life energy thus creates both the physical and the psychic components. Furthermore, according to this view, the activity of the organism, i.e. human life itself, consists of certain basic substances. In addition to blood and bodily fluids, which are important as carriers of Qi, these are the so-called *Three Treasures* (San Bao):

- Jing
- Qi
- Shen.

Until the birth of man, the Three Treasures still represent a unity, which is also referred to as the "prenatal aspect". After that, a separation gradually takes place. This corresponds to the Daoist guiding principle of constant transformation and change (cf. the explanations on *Yin and Yang* in Volume 3 of this series). However, there is an interaction between Jing, Qi and Shen, so that it is essential for health that they are in a close and harmonious relationship with each other.

A goal of Qi Gong is therefore to collect these three aspects, refine them and transform them back into their original state. This process of refinement and unification is also known as "Inner Alchemy".

Figures 1 and 2 show the Chinese characters for Jing, Qi and Shen and the connections between them.

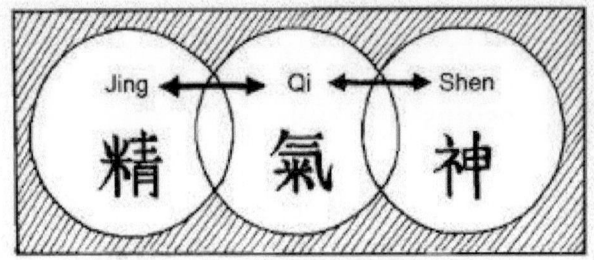

Figure 1

Figure 2

Jing

Jing can be translated as "essence". Literally translated, the Chinese characters mean "seed" and "purity".

In "Huangdi Neijing Suwen", the "Yellow Emperor's Classic of Internal Medicine" by Huang Di it is said: "Essence is the root of the body". This means that all human vitality, including thoughts, feelings and actions, first of all goes back to our physical substance. Only the basic physical basis allows us all further physical and mental developments. Jing thus stands for the most essential form, i.e. the source, of life energy. At the same time, the essence also has a formative power, since other things grow from it and it gives them structure.

A distinction must be made between the prenatal and the postnatal essence. This corresponds to what we postulated in Volume 2 of this series about the types of Qi. The prenatal part of the life essence is that which was given to us from birth and is stored in the kidneys. It is the driving force, the basis for human development. The postnatal essence is nourished by food, drink and breath and nourishes all physiological activities of the organism.

The physical development of a person is determined by the Jing. In childhood, the Jing provides growth and in young adults for maturation up to the peak of physical performance. With increasing age, it is gradually exhausted, after which physical deterioration begins. These symptoms can be accelerated by bad habits or delayed by a wise lifestyle. For the purpose of cultivating the Jing, among other things, a healthy diet, responsible use of alcohol and sexuality, avoiding emotional stress and practicing Qi Gong are recommended. This topic is dealt with in more detail in the special volume "The Qi Gong Diet".

Qi

Qi is the life force, the vital energy that pervades both solid matter and subtle forms of existence. Qi is the basis of inanimate things such as fire, water and earth, of animals and plants, of humans and of all life processes such as birth, growth and transformation. In addition to "energy", it is sometimes also translated as "breath" or "fluid", which is intended to make it clear that it is not subject to any specific form of appearance and can assume any physical state. This has already been explained in the previous volumes of this series.

The location of Qi is the Lower Dantian.

In connection with the Three Treasures, the concept of Qi represents the link between Jing and Shen, because it stands for movement and activity. This includes movements that can be seen as well as "stationary" movements that are very subtle or merely potential. While the essence initiates and drives the processes in our body, the life energy ensures their refinement and maintenance, warmth and protection. Qi is also associated with feeling.

One of the tasks of Qi in relation to humans is to keep the physiological functions of the organism in balance. Furthermore, the cultivation of Qi on the subtle level enables the Shen to be nourished. It is also said that together with the essence it forms the basis for the activity of the mind. Ultimately, body and mind should always be in harmony with each other.

Shen

Shen means spirit or mental energy. The Chinese characters used for this can be freely translated as "revealing a higher power". This means consciousness and reason, i.e. the ability to observe, interpret, differentiate and analyze one's own perceptions and emotions. The goal of an active, alert Shen is to gain control over one's emotions, to draw the right conclusions from perceptions and experiences, and to initiate creative and rational thought processes.

In traditional Chinese medicine, the heart is assumed to be the seat of the Shen. However, it also has a connection to the brain, where neurologically speaking, many of human mental processes take place.

In order to strengthen Shen, it is essential to prevent the mind from becoming exhausted and rather to give it enough rest. Chinese wisdom even says that the secret to a happy and long life lies in avoiding mental overload. Instead, it is advisable to remain calm and humble and not to waste one's mental faculties excessively on the gratification of desires and the attainment of material things and status symbols. Excessive rumination can also block the flow of Qi and weaken Shen.

The Roman poet Juvenal wrote:

"A healthy mind in a healthy body."

The best prerequisite for this is Qi Gong, which consists equally of movements, breathing and imagination.

The relationship between the Three Treasures

The classic sequence of steps as part of long-term Qi Gong training means that Jing is first built up, which then strengthens Qi and is finally refined into Shen. Jing develops into Qi and Qi into Shen, so to speak. A calm, clear mind can in turn control and favorably influence the functions of Jing and Qi. From a Daoist perspective, Shen can ultimately return to the primordial state of the universe, emptiness (Wu), and become one with the Dao (Way).

If, in the negative case, the essence is weakened (e.g. due to physical ailments, illness) or the Qi is blocked or used up (e.g. due to stress or overwork), there is a risk that mental performance will also decrease. Conversely, when Shen (mind) is dispersed, it cannot perform its function of regulating Jing and Qi.

TCM expert Ted Kaptchuk wrote on the subject:

"If you think of Jing as the source of life and Qi as the potential to activate and move, then Shen is the vitality in the human body that stands behind Jing and Qi. Moving and still movements are a manifestation of Qi, instinctive organic processes reflect Jing, human consciousness points to the presence of Shen."

The Three Treasures is a model that aims to explain and clarify the three basic components of life. As mentioned, they are by no means separate, stand-alone forces, but parts of a unit. It is an advantage for the Qi Gong practitioner to have basic knowledge of this principle of action.

How can we avoid diseases?

Since body and mind are inextricably linked via Qi, it is obvious that physical and mental illnesses can be mutually dependent. Physical suffering can have negative consequences for a person's psyche. Conversely, chronic illnesses of the body, for example, can be of a psychosomatic nature. The cause and at the same time the key to healing can be the Qi in these cases. If the Qi is weak or disordered, the symptoms of diseases can very easily arise.

In the more than two thousand year old "Classic of the Yellow Emperor on Internal Medicine" it's said:

"Many diseases are caused by disharmony of the Qi. In anger and trouble, Qi rises. When you are happy, it is sluggish. When sad, the Qi is discouraged. It retreats when it's cold. It escapes when it's hot. When frightened, things get confused. It is consumed during physical overhaul. With too much contemplation and brooding, it builds up. These are some of the reasons for Qi disorder."

The emotional, i.e. psychological factors mentioned there can disturb the free, harmonious flow of Qi and lead to congestion, blockages and an imbalance of Qi in a person's body.

This disrupts the functioning of the organism and diseases can develop and spread. On the other hand, the Qi can be so weakened and reduced by a continuously wrong way of life that it can no longer adequately cope with its tasks, such as supplying blood and organs with energy. For example, overwork, stress and excesses of various kinds can overtax the Qi. Imagine a vessel, such as a tank, filled with water, gas, or oil. If something is regularly removed from it, then you have to make sure you replenish it in good time, otherwise the supply will run out. It is the same with the Qi. In this way, most illnesses do not appear suddenly, but are initiated by prolonged mismanagement of life energy.

According to Traditional Chinese Medicine, we can certainly not avoid all diseases, but many, and in many cases heal them, if we are aware of the laws described above. Therefore, be careful with your energy reserves and, if possible, ensure that you only ever use as much of it as you are then able to regenerate. Also, try to avoid extreme states and emotions and, as a rule, take a sensible middle ground instead. Practicing Qi Gong helps you to always have enough Qi, to ensure a free flow of Qi and in general to develop the necessary mindfulness and sensitivity to recognize any harmful developments in good time.

Feng Shui

A teaching that is also known in the western world and deals with the laws and effectiveness of Qi is *Feng Shui* ("wind and water"). It is a theory of harmony that gives answers and hints as to how people can live better in harmony with their environment. The aim is to design living spaces such as the house, garden or workplace in such a way that as much fresh Qi as possible can circulate freely in them and the accumulation of used Qi is avoided. Feng Shui is based on Daoism and its individual philosophies, such as the existence of life energy, Yin and Yang, the 5 elementary phases of change, etc., which were described in the volumes of this series.

Below are five of the most basic laws of Feng Shui that you can consider to support Qi Gong if necessary. Most of the rules are universally applicable, whether it's a house, apartment, workspace, or a single room. Once you understand the key rules of Qi, you can easily make the appropriate adjustments as needed.

1. Let Qi into your home: The Qi follows the attention. If the path to your front door is clearly visible and the outside area is attractively designed, e.g. by putting up plants or other decorations, then a lot of Qi flows there on this path. Otherwise, light is the main carrier of Qi. If possible, plenty of sunlight should find its way into your home through window panes. Make sure that there are no mirrors pointing outwards in the entrance area, as they reflect the Qi back.

2.Open doors and passageways: In order for the light, as the carrier of Qi, to be able to move freely in the rooms, it makes sense to keep them open. Also ensure that all passages are easily accessible and not blocked. The bathroom is an exception, as it is naturally used for excretion and transportation. You can therefore keep the door closed. Incidentally, it is recommended that the areas of life are clearly separated from each other and that there is a visible division.

3.Distribute the Qi evenly with light, water and plants: Dark corners with little or no daylight can be illuminated with warm light from a lamp. In addition to light, water can be a suitable carrier of life energy. A nice indoor fountain would be a possibility, for example. Since plants also contain Qi, they are an excellent choice for letting an extra portion of Qi into your living space. Bare corners in particular can be enhanced in this way. In general, you should prefer round shapes, as they transport the Qi better than corners and edges.

4.Keeping things tidy: When rooms are overstuffed, superfluous things lie around and there is a general clutter, this disrupts the flow of Qi and used, negative Qi can build up and create an uncomfortable atmosphere. You should therefore rather rely on fewer, more accentuated accessories. Also make sure that everything is largely tidy, clear and clean. The same applies to plants, because here too it is important to remove faded flowers or dead leaves in good time.

5.Arrange the furniture correctly: Larger pieces of furniture should always be placed against the walls so that there is an open area in the middle through which life energy can flow. When it comes to seating, it is best if you have a solid wall behind you and you are looking towards the door. An exception is a desk or work table. A constant look out of the window, for example, can be distracting here under certain circumstances. In addition, you should definitely avoid standing in a draft between different doors or between doors and windows. This also applies to the bed in the bedroom. Colors should be chosen to match the room. In the bedroom, for example, you shouldn't choose a too flashy, stimulating tone, while this can be the case in the living room or the study.

Qi and plants

Plants provide humans with energy in the form of food and oxygen. Furthermore, plants – like animals – possess Qi, so it is possible for us to benefit from their life energy. For this it is enough if we stay close to plants and trees, become aware of their presence and get involved with it. In Japan, this has given rise to a trend known as "forest bathing". This means moving at a leisurely pace in a wooded area and perceiving the details of the surroundings with all your senses. One concentrates on smells, sounds or colors, such as the rustling of leaves or the scent of pine needles.

A simple Qi Gong exercise to do in a forest is to stand in front of a healthy tree and face your palms up toward the trunk and crown. You can remain in this position breathing calmly for as long as you like. Trees are able to absorb our used up Qi, clean it and give us fresh energy instead.

When we are near plants, we often feel content and connected to nature. But there are definitely differences between the individual types of plants. Some, such as the rose, belong to Yang and can stimulate our activity and imagination. Others, such as the orchid, belong to Yin and can provide calm and relaxation. To find out what is good for us, we should listen to our intuition and either stay in one place or, if necessary, look for another location.

Mindfulness

Mindfulness is a quality that is now increasingly being used in Western culture and science, e.g. in psychotherapy. In fact, the term goes back in particular to the Buddhist teachings of meditation. Buddha himself taught the "Noble Eightfold Path", the 7th tenet of which is "right mindfulness". There are even special meditations in Buddhism that are dedicated to mindfulness – in contrast to meditations that focus on concentration. Of course, mindfulness also plays a major role in Qi Gong practice.

Mindfulness can be described using the following characteristics:

-one is fully aware of what is going on in one's mind
-one is mindful of one's own body
-one is mindful of one's own feelings and sensations
-one is mindful of one's state of mind (alert, focused, confused, etc.)
-one is mindful of the objects of one's mind, i.e. all objects that are presently perceived
-one does not think about the perceptions and does not evaluate them.

Mindfulness is therefore a special state of consciousness and perception that goes beyond mere attention.

Before we begin our Qi Gong practice, we always try to put ourselves in the so-called Qi Gong state. This should help us to leave the worries of everyday life behind for a while and focus better on the training ahead. When we then do a Qi Gong exercise, we are completely in the here and now and pay attention to what is going on inside us. If we find that our attention is deviating or that our body is giving us certain signals, then we notice this, make adjustments if necessary and just keep practicing.

A significant feature of mindfulness, then, is that you focus entirely on the moment without constantly thinking about the past and the future. Nor should we constantly evaluate everything and everyone and weigh up the pros and cons. Just be aware of your surroundings as they are the moment you are in, and be aware of your thoughts, feelings, and physical reactions.

Anyone who succeeds in showing mindfulness in everyday life is not so easily guided by sudden emotions and creates a distance between themselves and any problems, worries and needs. This leads to an increase in serenity, well-being and a slowing down of life.

Right mindfulness in the sense of the Buddha's teachings comes about all by itself over time through Qi Gong training. The combination of movement, breathing and imagination is ideally suited to positively and sustainably influencing our everyday consciousness.

How do I know that my Qi Gong training is successful?

The positive effects of the Qi Gong exercises appear immediately and not only over time. However, with increasing practice experience, the speed, precision and capacity of Qi absorption will continue to improve. Furthermore, our sensitivity increases so that we perceive the characteristics of the energy flow more easily. For example, a pleasant feeling of warmth in the hands tells us that the Qi is flowing in us and doing its work.

Life energy is something natural, and therefore the practitioner should always be careful to show easiness and naturalness. If you feel good while practicing Qi Gong, then the health effects are also good. Especially after training you should clearly feel the fresh supply of Qi in the body and the better permeability of the meridians.

After some time of repeated training, you will see clearer results, because the gain of physical energy and mental freshness increases performance and joie de vivre and ailments are noticeably reduced. At the same time, the boundaries between the time of practice and non-practice (everyday life) will blur over time as the correct form of movement, breathing and awareness (e.g. inner smile, mindfulness) are internalized unconsciously. Once we have gotten this far, we practice Qi Gong practically anytime and anywhere and benefit from it – whether we think about it or not.

If, in individual cases, you feel exhausted while practicing or even experience a headache or something similar, then take a break and continue the training on another day. Don't force anything and give yourself the time you need.

Above all, listen to your intuition. This always proves to be a wise advisor. So sometimes it's better to gather your experience and let things "take care of themselves".

Practical part

Bone Marrow-Qi Gong

The importance of the exercises

The bone marrow plays an important role in Traditional Chinese Medicine (TCM) because it is responsible for blood production. It is also believed to have a close relationship with the kidneys, which in turn are an important storage location for Qi.

Macroscopically, a distinction can be made between red and yellow bone marrow. Healthy bones contain more red bone marrow. While yellow bone marrow consists of fat deposits ("fat marrow"), red bone marrow is used for blood formation, i.e. it contains precursor cells of blood cells (see Figure 3).

Bone marrow Qi Gong ensures that the proportion of red bone marrow is increased and the proportion of fat in the bones is reduced. In this way, blood production is increased, tissues are nourished with oxygen and blood circulation is stimulated throughout the body. The inner character of the exercises also increases the sensitivity of the body and the ability to listen to one's own body. In addition, the exercises – like all Qi Gong practices – serve to bring fresh Qi into the body, eliminate used Qi, remove blockages and initiate the process of inner alchemy – Jing, Qi and Shen.

Bones have a porous structure and are therefore generally permeable, e.g. for oxygen, blood and nutrients. It can definitely be compared to a sponge (see Figure 4).

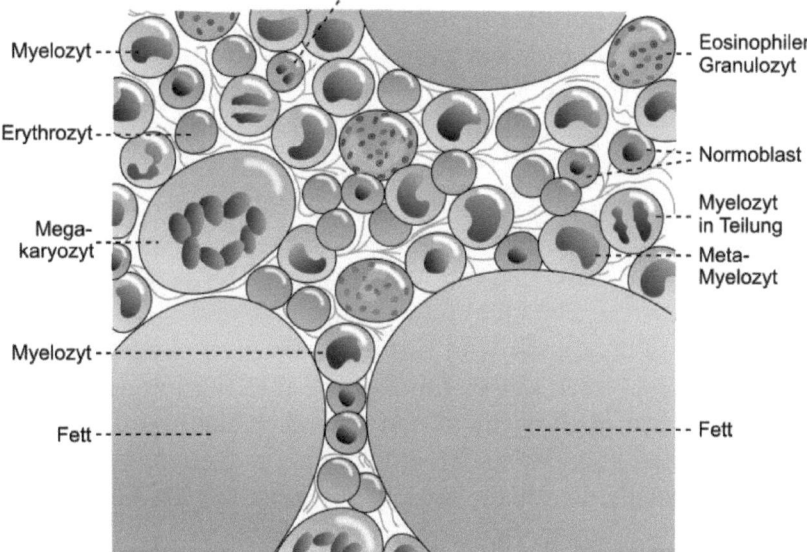

Figure 3

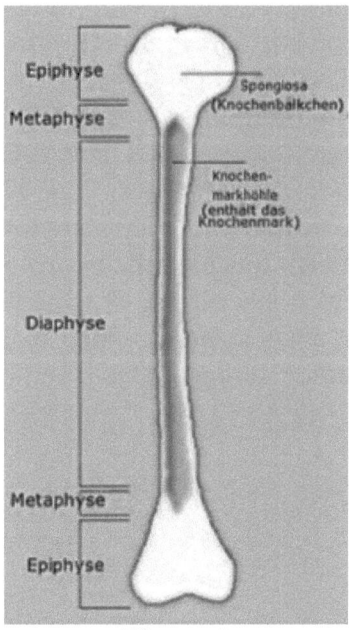

Figure 4

All Bone Marrow Qi Gong exercises are internal exercises (Nei Dan), i.e. our body is not moving on the outside but is moving on the inside. Every Qi Gong exercise consists of body (movement, posture) + breathing + imagination. For the purpose of strengthening and purifying the bone marrow, imagination takes an essential part. This means that we focus our mental attention primarily on evoking the appropriate imagination. You can imagine the flow of Qi as bright or white light radiation.

One of the basic rules of working with Qi is that imagination and thought move Qi. The Qi in turn moves the blood.

When you breathe in with Bone Breathing or Bone Compression, you will feel clear, fresh air, or Qi, rushing into the interstices of the body, expanding and opening them. On the other hand, you will feel a slight contraction as you exhale. Breathing should always be slow and smooth and not associated with any muscle tension.

Before beginning the practice of bone marrow Qi Gong, it is appropriate to put yourself in the so-called Qi Gong state with the *3 preparatory exercises* Rubbing your eyebrows – Listening – Creating the inner smile (see volume 1 of the series). It is important that you are in an undisturbed environment that is at a comfortable temperature and that you are in a state of relaxation and receptivity. This means you are ready to leave everyday life behind for a while.

For all of the exercises discussed here, it is recommended to assume a lying position. You lie on your back, your eyes are closed, your thumbs are ideally pointing up and your palms are inward, so that your fingertips are free in space and not touching the floor.

Also, you should not wear shoes to make it easier for the toes to absorb Qi. If lying down is not possible for some reason, the exercises can be carried out either sitting or standing.

Bone breathing

Bone breathing is usually performed at the beginning of Bone Marrow Qi Gong. This is because this exercise improves the body's receptivity and permeability to Qi, which is an ideal preparation for further practice. In addition, the time required is relatively small. Of course, Bone breathing can also be done as a standalone exercise, as it has the ability to strengthen bones, stimulate their function, and improve overall blood circulation. As a side effect, the exercise provides deep relaxation and a release of muscle tension.

As with all three of the Bone Marrow Qi Gong exercises discussed here, begin by lying comfortably. The eyes are closed.

Alternatively, there is also the option of doing the exercise in a standing position – e.g. the *tree* (see Volume 3 of this series). However, it is easier to relax and concentrate on the necessary imaginations in a lying position, which is why such a position is generally recommended,

With regard to breathing, it is generally advantageous, i.e. for most Qi Gong exercises as well as in everyday life, to practice *normal abdominal breathing* (Buddhist breathing) with a slow exhalation. In this way, the absorbed energy builds up defense Qi in the outer parts of the body, which strengthens our immune system.

However, with bone marrow Qi Gong, it is important to focus on the inhalation instead. With the help of a deep inhalation, the Qi is transported to the inner, more difficult-to-reach areas of the body, such as the bone marrow. This effect can be enhanced by engaging in *reverse abdominal breathing*, also known as Daoist breathing. This means that you breathe in slowly and consciously while contracting the abdominal wall. When you exhale, your stomach returns to its usual position. For detailed instructions on the different breathing methods, see Volume 2 of this series.

The practice of Bone breathing consists of taking Qi into the body on the inhale and releasing it out again on the exhale. You breathe deeply into the middle of the bones, which is associated with a feeling of expansion (see Figures 5 and 6).

When you exhale, the Qi is released to the outside again, which is associated with a feeling of contraction.

Here you go through 5 different body areas one after the other. These are:

-arms
-legs
-spine
-head
-ribs.

Bone compression follows the same sequence. The only difference is that with Bone breathing you should also divide your arms and legs into hands, lower and upper arms, or feet, lower legs and thighs. This will improve their perception in each area.

For each area of the body, you can repeat Bone breathing as many times as you like, depending on the amount of time you want. Over time you will be able to perceive the feeling of Qi flowing deep into the body faster and more clearly.

<u>The instructions</u>

On the first inhalation, imagine that a great quantity of Qi is being carried from the universe into your hands through your fingertips. This is generally accompanied by a cool feeling. As you exhale, imagine the energy being brought back out the same way. This is generally accompanied by a warm feeling.

On the next inhalation, breathe in the Qi through your fingertips and down into your forearm. On the exhale, release it back out.

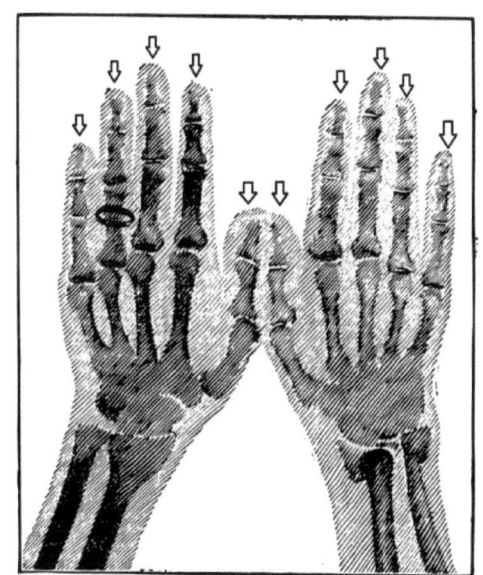
Figure 5

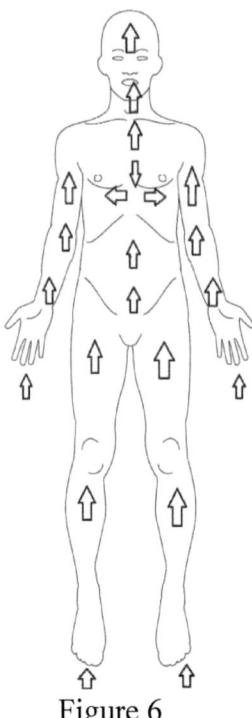
Figure 6

Then, as you breathe in, guide the Qi through your fingertips up into your upper arm. When you exhale, the energy is brought back outside of the body.

Next, do the legs in the same way. To do this, breathe in through your toes and first direct the Qi into your feet. When you breathe out, the energy flows out of the body again. Then repeat the procedure with the lower legs and finally the thighs.

The area of the body that we will focus on below is the spine. To do this, breathe in Qi through your fingertips and toes at the same time. Thus the Qi flows into the spine from above through the fingertips, arms and shoulders and from below through the toes, legs and pelvis. The two streams meet either just below the collarbone or in the middle of the spine at vertebra T11.

On the exhale, the two processes are reversed until the Qi has left the body. You can repeat Bone breathing in the spine area several times before moving on to the next step.

The next part of the exercise is to move the Qi to the head as you inhale. For this purpose, you first proceed in such a way that you direct the Qi through your fingertips, arms and shoulders and at the same time through your toes, legs and pelvis to the area of the shoulder blades (or the lower-lying vertebra T11). At this point they unite both streams and then rise together until they fill the head area. When you breathe out, the energy flows out as usual along the same path. With the head in particular, it is important that the Qi does not remain there longer than necessary and that it is lowered again after the end of the exercise step or at the latest the entire exercise.

Finally, the Qi is breathed into the ribs and breastbone. To do this, repeat the already known path that the energy should take one more time. Imagine the Qi moving through the fingertips, arms and shoulders, toes, legs and pelvis to the top of the spine. The two tracks then unite and climb up to the head. From there the energy moves back down to the 12 pairs of ribs and the sternum. When you exhale, the Qi flows out of the body the same way.

Especially for the last parts of the exercise it is necessary to breathe in slowly, otherwise you will have trouble imagining the entire course of the Qi. You should be aware that the Qi flows rather leisurely. In addition, the success of the exercise is inevitably related to the power of your imagination. As with all things, practice makes perfect here, so breathing and imagination will gradually harmonize better and better.

You can either move on to the final exercises at this point if you want to end your exercise session, or you can move on to another exercise like Bone compression. In addition to the above-mentioned traditional instructions for Bone breathing, there is another variant that you can devote yourself to afterwards. This consists of doing Bone breathing simultaneously throughout the body, using what is known as *body breathing*.

Body breathing means imagining that the Qi is sucked in and absorbed with all the pores of the body at the same time. For this exercise, stay in reverse abdominal breathing with the focus on the inhalation. With each inhalation, imagine that Qi from all over the universe is being absorbed through every pore in the body and going as deep as it can into the bone marrow. When you breathe out, the Qi is let out again in the same way. You can repeat this process for as long as you want and feel comfortable.

Bone compression

Bone compression is very commonly performed after Bone breathing. Both exercises are related in structure, with Bone compression being significantly more extensive. Of course, you can also do this exercise on your own.

Here, too, the starting position is a comfortable, lying position, with the edges of the hands resting loosely on the floor so that the fingertips are in the air as much as possible. The eyes are closed (see Figures 7 and 8).

Ideally, we use reverse abdominal breathing for breathing. If you still have difficulties with this at first, you can stick with normal abdominal breathing. In any case, during the breathing cycles, the focus should be on the inhalation, which means that it happens slowly, carefully, and completely. Imaginations are also generated during inhalation.

During the exercise, the 5 body areas already mentioned in Bone breathing are dealt with one after the other: arms – legs – spine – head - ribs (see Figure 9).

Furthermore, three individual exercise steps are carried out for each body area. These are the following:

1. Spiral
2. Pack
3. Squeeze.

Figure 10 shows a corresponding sketch using the example of the right arm.

By "spiral" is meant inhaling Qi through fingers and toes. The difference from Bone breathing is that you direct the breath not only into the bones, but into all areas of the body. In addition, you should imagine the energy flows spiraling like a screw movement. The Qi entering the body through the fingers and toes on the right side moves clockwise around the bones. The Qi that enters the body through the fingers and toes on the left side moves counterclockwise around the bones. In this way, the space inside the body is optimally filled.

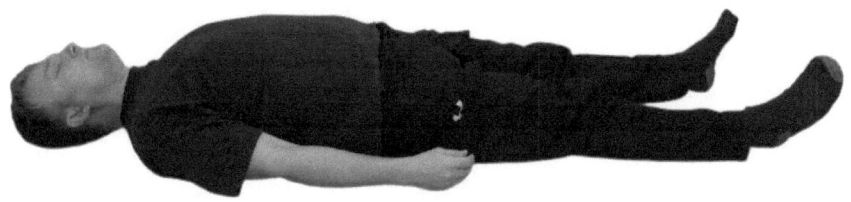

Figure 7

Figure 8

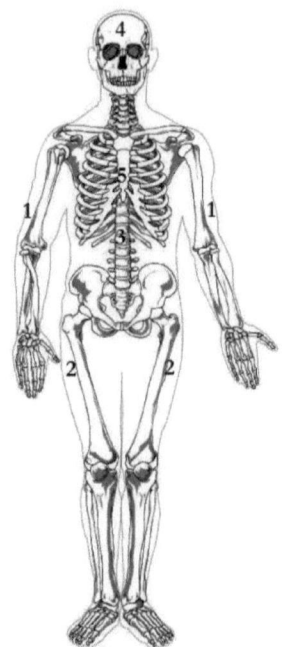

Figure 9

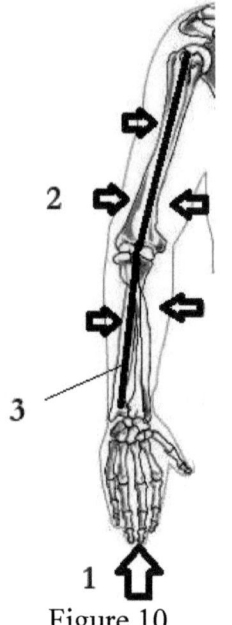

Figure 10

"Packing" or "packing in" occurs when you feel that the body area you are attending to is well filled with Qi. To do this, during the following inhalation, imagine that the Qi is being concentrated and condensed immediately around the bones. The energy is packed deeper into the body, so to speak, through the muscles and other tissues. As I said, this is a purely mental process, i.e. the power of imagination is used.

"Squeezing", on the other hand, is a physical action. To do this, after breathing in again, hold your breath and briefly tense all the muscles in the affected body region. As a result, the Qi previously concentrated around the bones is transported deep into the bones and bone marrow, or squeezed. However, be careful not to sustain the contraction for too long so that overexertion or energy congestion does not occur. With some experience in Qi Gong you will quickly develop a feel for it. In general, one should not hold one's breath, but – analogous to the Daoist teachings of Yin and Yang – always let it flow freely. In this case, however, it is advisable to pause as an exception, since this is the best way to bring the Qi deep into the bones without loss.

The instructions

Bone Compression begins with you breathing fresh Qi from the Universe in a spiral through your fingertips into your arms. Unlike Bone breathing, this time you breathe directly into your whole arms. After concentrating on a slow inhalation, the exhalation happens naturally and without any imagination. Instead, dwell your attention on the arms and the Qi that is already there. Your goal for now is to collect and store as much energy as possible in your arms. For example, you can breathe in for three breath cycles, or until you have a clear feeling of Qi in your arms.

Then, on the next inhalation, as described above, imagine the Qi in your arms being condensed and concentrated so that it packs tightly around the bones.

The subsequent inhalation is without action. Then stop breathing and tighten your arm muscles. You don't have to imagine anything. It is enough if you are aware that with this procedure the Qi is transported to the bone marrow. If, after a few seconds, you feel that too much effort is needed, relax your body again and allow yourself to exhale.

Then repeat the same three steps with your legs. Inhale slowly and spirally into them until they are energized, on the next inhale imagine the Qi being carried through the flesh to the edge of the bones, and finally hold your breath and perform a muscle contraction through, so that the Qi is pressed into the bones to the marrow.

The third body area is the spine. To do this, breathe equally through your hands and toes, whereupon the Qi enters the torso through the arms and shoulders on the one hand and the legs and pelvis on the other. As you exhale, focus on keeping the energy stored in that area. After a while, on the inhale, perform the packing, imagining that the energy is being carried through the tissues close to the bones of the spine.

After the subsequent inhalation, hold the exhalation and allow the muscles of the core area to contract for a short time. The Qi is squeezed into the bone marrow. On the next inhalation, the Qi is again inhaled equally through the fingers and toes. The two streams of energy unite below the shoulder girdle, now rise up to the head and fill it out. When exhaling, the Qi remains in the head area. At some point you will breathe in and imagine the Qi condensing in the immediate vicinity of the skull. Then you hold your breath and momentarily tense the muscles of your head, which induces Qi into the bone marrow there.

Finally, the focus is on the ribs and the breastbone (sternum). Strive to inhale slowly, imagining the flow of Qi through the hands, arms, shoulders and spine, and through the feet, legs, pelvis and spine until the two streams join below the shoulder girdle. From there the energy first rises to the head and then descends again until it fills the chest. Repeat this a few times. On the next inhalation, visualize the Qi being concentrated around the bones. After that, inhale again, hold your breath, and perform muscle contraction to squeeze the Qi into the bone marrow.

Similar to the explanations for Bone breathing, you can end the Bone compression at this point and move on to one of the concluding exercises or carry out an additional variant. You use body breathing again and devote yourself to the whole body in a single exercise step.

To do this, breathe in Qi through all the pores of the body at the same time, like a sponge absorbing water. As you breathe out, make sure that the energy stays in the body and is collected there. When you have concentrated enough Qi in the body in this way, breathe in again and, by the power of your imagination, pack the energy through muscles and tissues to your bones. After the next inhalation, stop breathing and contract the muscles of the whole body for a few seconds, so that the Qi is pressed into the bones.

Bone marrow washing

This exercise is called the *Bone marrow washing*. It has an inner character and relies solely on the imagination. It is usually performed in a comfortable, lying position (supine position). Alternatively, it can of course also be performed standing (e.g. *the tree* pose) or sitting. In any case, the body remains completely relaxed the whole time.

Also, unlike *Bone breathing* and *Bone compression*, you don't need to give special importance to breathing. Just breathe slowly and calmly in normal abdominal breathing.

As far as the use of imagination is concerned, it is important that it is purposeful and lively, but not forced, tense or too strained. Rather, it is a matter of sensing and observing, which you will be able to do better, more satisfactorily and more effectively over time. It is also not necessary for you to know and understand the exact appearance and location of the organs or the sounds inside the body. A good basic knowledge of human anatomy is sufficient.

Figure 11 shows some of the major organs in our body. During the Bone marrow washing, the bones, meat and skin, among other things, are separated from one another. You will go through the following three areas one after the other: arms, legs and spine. Figure 12 shows X-rays of an arm.

The goals of Bone marrow washing are, of course, strengthening the bones, stimulating bone marrow production, improving blood circulation, dissolving energetic blockages and supporting the nervous system. A special feature of this exercise is that Qi and breath are not only directed into the interior of the bones, but also specifically into the spaces between bones, muscles, skin and hair. Almost all bodily processes benefit from this, and vitality and joie de vivre are increased.

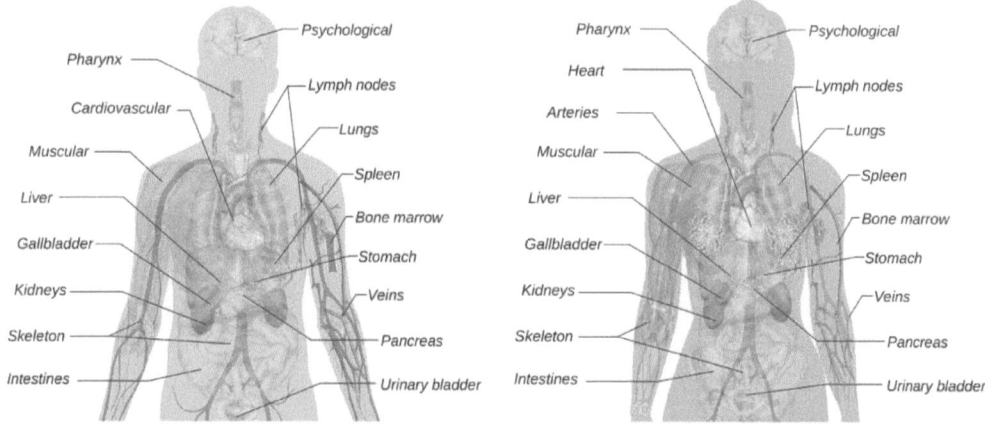

Figure 11

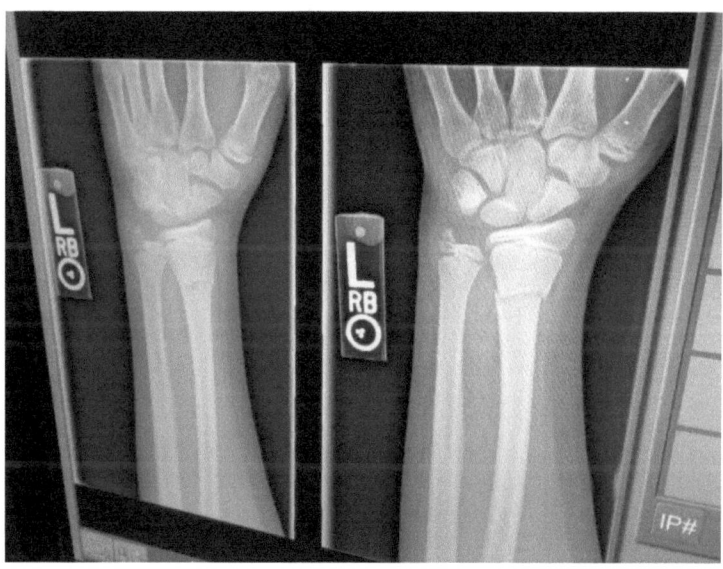

Figure 12

The instructions

As said above, initiate the Bone marrow washing sequentially for the arms, legs, and spine. The imagined process always consists of the following 8 exercise steps, which are also referred to as *goals*:

1. open the joints
2. concentrate the bone marrow
3. separate the bones from the flesh
4. separate the flesh from the skin
5. raise the body hair
6. see inner course and structure
7. hear inner course and structure
8. imagine the correct alignment, color and function of the organs.

Only do each step once for a total of 24 practice steps. Proceed slowly and carefully, then move smoothly and fluidly from one step to the next.

Begin by imagining that all the joints in your arms are being pulled open. You start at the shoulders, move on to the elbow joint, wrist and finally the finger joints. Feel how gently and carefully some space is created in all joints.

Next, take your mind deep inside your body to the bone marrow. Concentrate and condense the marrow, starting with the fingers and working up to the shoulders.

After that, use your imagination to separate the bones from the flesh that surrounds them. This creates free space in which the Qi can spread. The course is now again from the shoulders to the fingertips.

Now proceed according to the same principle by separating the soft tissue from the skin above it. Start with your fingers and move on to your hands, forearms, upper arms, and shoulders.

The next step is to raise all the body hair. Feel – from your shoulders to your fingers – how every tiny hair stands up, creating space between skin and hair.

Now imagine the inner course and structure of the arms from fingers to shoulders. Try to see, or rather feel, the individual vessels, the blood, the muscles, the marrow, etc. in your mind's eye.

Then move your attention back from your shoulders to your fingers, this time striving to hear the organs, blood, Qi and inner workings of the body, so to speak with your "inner hearing".

Finally, from your fingers to your shoulders, visualize that all your organs, muscles, tendons, bones, blood, skin, and hair are healthy and strong. Imagine with conviction that the alignment, function, color and shape of all parts of the body are just right and desirable.

Next, repeat the same process with your legs. Start at the hips and imagine that all the joints are being pulled open up to the toes. Feel how space for Qi and breath is created in the hip, knee, foot and toe joints.

After that, move on to concentrating and condensing the bone marrow. Start at the toes and continue up to the hips.

Then, using your imagination, separate the bones from the flesh, i.e. all the soft tissue. Do this from your hips to your toes.

Likewise, you then separate the flesh from the skin that covers it. The course this time is again from the toes, over feet, lower thighs, thighs to the hips.

In the following, visualize that all body hairs stand up individually. Work from hips to toes.

The next step is to use your "inner view" to look at the internal flow and structure of your legs. Start at the toes and work your way down to your hips. Imagine vessels, blood, muscles, etc. in front of your inner eye.

Now move your attention again from your hips to your toes, this time trying to hear the inner workings of organs, blood, Qi, etc.

Finally, as far as the legs are concerned, revisit the inner path from toes to hips. On this occasion they visualize that the alignment, color and function of the organs, muscles, tendons, bones, blood, skin and hair are healthy, strong and therefore just right.

The spinal exercise sequence begins by pulling open all joints from the tailbone to the back of the head.

After that, concentrate the bone marrow in the spine in the reverse direction, i.e. from the back of the head (base of the skull) to the tailbone.

Then, using your imagination to separate the bones from the flesh, again work your way up from your tailbone to the back of your head.

The separation of the flesh from the skin, which you do in the next step, is again carried out downwards from the back of the head to the tailbone.

Next, in the trunk area, raise all the body hair using your imagination. Start at the tailbone and slowly work your way up to the back of your head.

Next, do the "inner view". Follow the inner course of the torso from the back of the head to the coccyx and look at and feel the vessels, blood, muscles, etc. located there.

The next step is to use your "inner hearing" to trace the inner course of the trunk and spine, listening and feeling the workings of organs, blood, qi, etc. Work from your tailbone to the back of your head.

Finally visualize the inner course of the torso and spine from the back of the head to the coccyx. The alignment, color and function of the organs, muscles, tendons, bones, blood, skin and hair are perfectly healthy, strong and exactly as they should be.

Summary of the exercises

Bone breathing

-reverse abdominal breathing with concentration on the inhalation

1. Arms

-inhale Qi through the fingers into the hands, release it again on the exhale; to repeat

-inhale Qi through your fingers into your forearms, release it on the exhale; to repeat

-inhale Qi through the fingers into the upper arms, release it again while exhaling; to repeat

2. Legs

-breathe Qi into the feet through the toes and release it on the exhale; to repeat

-inhale Qi through the toes into the lower legs, release it again on the exhale; to repeat

-inhale Qi through the toes into the thighs, release it again on the exhale; to repeat

3. Spine

-inhale Qi from above into the spine through fingers, arms and shoulders; simultaneously inhale Qi through toes, legs and pelvis from below into spine; released on exhalation; to repeat

4. Head

-inhale Qi through fingers, arms, shoulders and spine on the one hand and through toes, legs, pelvis and spine on the other hand to below the shoulder girdle and from there to the head; released on exhalation; to repeat

5. Ribs and sternum

-inhale Qi through fingers, arms, shoulders and spine on the one hand and through toes, legs, pelvis and spine on the other hand to below the shoulder girdle, from there to the head and finally down to the ribs and sternum; released on exhalation; to repeat

6. Body breathing

-while inhaling, inhale Qi with all pores of the body; released on exhalation; to repeat

Bone Compression
-reverse abdominal breathing with concentration on the inhalation
1. Arms
-inhale Qi spirally into the arms through the fingers; exhale without imagination; repeat (spiral)
-when inhaling, imagining that the Qi is being concentrated close to the bones (pack); exhale without imagination
-inhale, hold your breath while tensing your arm muscles to push Qi into the bone marrow (squeeze)
2. Legs
-inhale Qi spirally through the toes into the legs; exhale without imagination; repeat (spiral)
-when inhaling, imagining that the Qi is being concentrated close to the bones (pack); exhale without imagination
-inhale, hold your breath while tensing your leg muscles to push Qi into the bone marrow (squeeze)
3. Spine
-inhale Qi spirally from above into the torso through fingers, arms and shoulders; simultaneously inhale Qi spirally through toes, legs and pelvis from below into the torso; exhale without imagination; repeat (spiral)
-when inhaling, imagining that the Qi is being concentrated close to the bones (pack); exhale without imagination
-inhale, holding your breath while contracting the core muscles to push Qi into the bone marrow (squeeze)
4. Head
-inhale Qi through fingers, arms, shoulders and spine on the one hand and through toes, legs, pelvis and spine on the other in a spiral way to below the shoulder girdle and from there to the head; exhale without imagination; repeat (spiral)
-when inhaling, imagining that the Qi is being concentrated close to the bones (pack); exhale without imagination
-inhale, hold your breath while contracting the muscles of your head so that Qi is pushed into the bone marrow (squeeze)

5. Ribs and sternum
-inhale Qi through fingers, arms, shoulders and spine on the one hand and through toes, legs, pelvis and spine on the other in a spiral way to below the shoulder girdle, from there to the head and finally down to the ribs and sternum; exhale without imagination; repeat (spiral)
-on inhalation imagining that the Qi is being concentrated close to the bones (pack), exhaling without imagining
-inhale, holding your breath while contracting the muscles of the chest to push Qi into the bone marrow (squeeze)

6. Body breathing
-while inhaling, inhale Qi with all pores of the body; exhale without imagination; repeat (spiral)
-on inhalation imagining that the Qi is being concentrated close to the bones (pack), exhaling without imagining
-inhale, hold your breath while tensing all body muscles so that Qi is pushed into the bone marrow (squeeze)

Bone marrow washing
-perform each exercise step (gate) once
1. Arms:
-open the joints from shoulders to fingers
-concentrate the bone marrow from fingers to shoulders
-separate the bones from the flesh from shoulders to fingers
-separate the flesh from the skin from fingers to shoulders
-raise body hair from shoulders to fingers
-see the inner course and structure of the arms from fingers to shoulders (inner view)
-hear the inner course and structure of the arms from shoulders to fingers (inner hearing)
-imagine the alignment, color and function of the organs from the fingers to the shoulders and realize that they are just right.

2.Legs:
-open the joints from hips to toes
-concentrate the bone marrow from toes to hips
-separate the bones from the flesh from hips to toes
-separate the flesh from the skin from toes to hips
-raise body hair from hips to toes
-see the inner course and structure of the legs from toes to hips (inner view)
-hear the inner course and structure of the legs from hips to toes (inner hearing)
-imagine the alignment, color and function of organs from toes to hips and realize that they are just right.

3.Spine:
-open the joints from the coccyx to the back of the head
-concentrate the bone marrow from the back of the head to the coccyx
-separate the bones from the flesh from the tailbone to the back of the head
-separate the flesh from the skin from the back of the head to the tailbone
-raise the body hair from the tailbone to the back of the head
-see the inner course and structure of the spine and torso from the back of the head to the coccyx (inner view)
-hear the inner course and structure of the spine and torso from the coccyx to the back of the head (inner hearing)
-imagine the alignment, color and function of the organs from the back of the head to the tailbone and realize that they are just right.

Final exercises

Once you have practiced one or more of the Bone Marrow Qi Gong exercises, you can complete the final exercises described below. Return to normal abdominal breathing.

To stretch oneself

If you've practiced in a lying position, begin by gently moving your limbs. Stretch and straighten your arms and legs and loll after staying on your pad for as long as you feel comfortable. When you find that your circulation has regained its momentum, stand up slowly.

The rocking horse

Now take the neutral Wuji stance again. Imagine that your feet are anchored deep into the earth, analogous to the roots of a tree. Alternatively, you can take a slightly wider stance and let your palms face down.

Then begin to alternately shift your body weight to the left and right. You can imagine that your shoulders (Jianjing acupuncture point) want to approach your soles (Yongquan points). Do the rocking gently and feel the Qi, blood and bodily fluids moving from side to side like a wave. Repeat the process for as long as you like (see Figures 13 and 14).

The circulation of the Qi is stimulated with the help of the rocking horse exercise.

Self-massage and tapping

Now take the neutral Wuji stance again. Imagine that your feet are anchored deep into the earth, analogous to the roots of a tree. Alternatively, you can take a slightly wider stance and let your palms face down.

Stimulating the Qi Gong points (acupuncture points) and other areas of the body is an ideal means of stimulating the flow of Qi, dissolving blockages and deepening and consolidating the success of the Bone marrow washing. You can do this by self-massage or tapping your own body. A good option is to combine both methods.

Figure 13

Figure 14

During self-massage, the appropriate areas of the body are rubbed with the hands. You should apply some pressure while doing this, as it is a stimulating practice, unlike a relaxation massage. However, you should always proceed with ease and not strain your hands and arms excessively.

When tapping, the hands are formed into bowls and the fingers are laid loosely together. Here, too, make sure that you do not use too much force when performing the tapping movements, so that you avoid overstraining the stimulated areas. With a little experience and the power of intuition, you will surely succeed. Devote yourself to the individual areas for as long as you like and it seems helpful to you.

The areas to be treated sequentially by self-massage or tapping are the following:

-face
-skullcap
-occiput
-shoulder belt
-outsides of the arms
-inside of the arms
-breast
-belly
-waist
-the back
-outsides of the legs
-insides of the legs.

When rubbing or tapping the face, one hand can be devoted to one side of the face at a time (see Figure 15).

When rubbing the skullcap, it is a good idea to use your fingertips (see Figure 16).

At the back of the head, the two hands can alternate and tap or stroke downwards one after the other.

You can grasp the shoulder girdle or the upper back area from above with both hands as well as you can.

The inside of the arms (see Figure 17) are worked from top to bottom, i.e. from the shoulders to the hands.

The outer sides of the arms are worked from the bottom up, i.e. from the hands to the shoulders.

From the chest you can seamlessly transition down to the abdomen including the Lower Dantian (see Figure 18).

Pat or massage the waist from bottom to top.

When tapping or massaging your lower back, start at the tailbone and then work your way up as far as your mobility allows. It helps if you lean forward a little while doing this.

For the outside of the legs, work from top to bottom (see also the 6th Brocade while standing in Volume 1 of the series).

For the inside of the legs, work from bottom to top.

A recommended option is to work on the face, skullcap and back of the head with self-massage and the other areas of the body with tapping.

Finally, you can place both palms on the Lower Dantian, close your eyes and continue to breathe quietly for a while without any special imagination. In this way the Qi is again collected and stored in the Lower Dantian.

The Lower Dantian is located a few centimeters below the belly button inside the body. Women put their left hand on their right. Men put their right hand on their left. See also the detailed explanations in the previous volumes of the series.

Figure 15

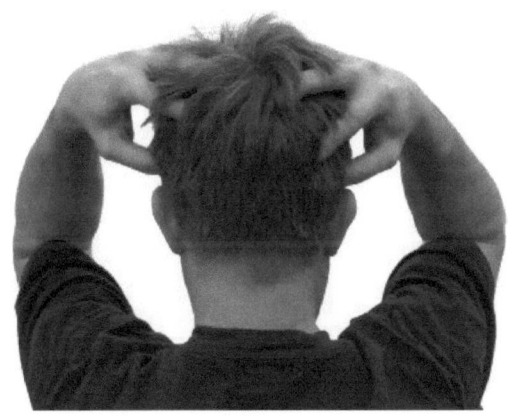

Figure 16

Figure 17

Figure 18

Embryonic breathing

The goals of Embryonic breathing

The so-called *Embryonic breathing* is a meditation in which breathing and especially imagination are important. It is one of the traditional elements of Qi Gong teaching. The term is based on the breathing that an embryo performs in the mother's womb, which indicates that in this way a return to nature and to the neutral, unadulterated state of things (Wuji) should take place.

The first goal of the exercise is to bring as much Qi as possible into our body and store it immediately in the Lower Dantian. It is important that Qi never rises and remains in the upper body for a long period of time, otherwise this will confuse and exhaust the mind, increasing blood pressure and heart rate, among other things. Consequently, whenever we have an increased need for life energy, we will be able to fall back on a sufficiently large supply in the Lower Dantian. From Yang point of view, the body becomes stronger and more durable.

Furthermore, a connection between the Upper Dantian (Shen = spirit) and the Lower Dantian is created through the imagination, which we use in Embryonic breathing. The declared goal is to calm the mind, to bring it into a natural, unencumbered state over time and to unite it with the Qi in the Lower Dantian. See also the explanations for the 3 treasures in this volume. From a Yin point of view, the mind is purified and becomes more efficient.

Finally, with the help of this meditation exercise, the breathing itself becomes visibly deeper, finer and more subtle. Among other things, this promotes the circulation of Qi in the body.

The practice of Embryonic breathing

The content of the exercise is that during meditation you inhale Qi into your body and take it in a direct path to Lower Dantian. The Lower Dantian is located about 3 cm below the navel inside the body.

The imagination used in Embryonic breathing also requires knowledge of one of the Extraordinary Meridians, namely the *Chong Mai*. This runs in a vertical line inside the body from the pelvis to the mouth area and is connected to the spinal cord. It meets all 12 main meridians and is therefore also called "The Sea of 12 Meridians" or simply "Central Channel" (see Figure 19 and Volume 4 of the series).

The exercise is generally performed while seated. You can use a seat cushion, for example. Volume 4 of this series describes some suitable sitting postures, such as the *Burmese seat*, the *Cross-legged seat* or the *Heel seat*. The body is kept natural and relaxed the whole time. According to the 70% rule, pain or excessive straining of muscles, tendons and ligaments should be avoided at all costs. The tip of the tongue is placed on the palate. The eyes are closed (see Figure 20).

With regard to the position of the hands, the following is recommended: place your hands on top of each other in your lap so that the palms are facing up and the tips of the thumbs are touching. Men traditionally put their left hand in, or up in this pose, and their right hand out, or down in this pose. With women it is the opposite. This is an outflow of the Daoist Yin/Yang philosophy.

Alternatively, you can place your hands directly on the lower abdomen (similar to the classic final Qi Gong exercise) or use one of the hand positions described in the other volumes in the series.

With regard to the exercise technique used, the following alternatives are possible:

-Buddhist or Daoist method
-Concentration on the inhalation or exhalation.

The *Buddhist method* of Embryo breathing involves a specific imagination that occurs solely during inhalation and the use of normal abdominal breathing.

In normal abdominal breathing, the abdominal wall and lower back bulge outward as you inhale, while the abdomen pushes down against the intestines. On the exhale, there is a return to the initial state (see also the instructions in Volume 1 of the series).

As you inhale, imagine Qi being channeled through all the pores of the body, first into the Chong Mai and from there straight to the Lower Dantian. The exhalation happens without imagination.

The *Daoist method* of Embryo breathing is connected to a similar concept, but here it is divided into inhalation and exhalation. Besides reverse abdominal breathing is used.

In reverse abdominal breathing, the abdominal wall and lower back contract as you inhale, while the abdomen pulls up. On the exhale, there is a return to the initial state as usual (see also the instructions in Volume 1 of the series).

When inhaling, the idea is that Qi is being breathed into the Chong Mai through all the pores of the body. As you exhale, imagine the Qi descending from there to the Lower Dantian.

The Daoist variant generally has a stronger effect when done correctly and can therefore be recommended for advanced users. However, if you like the Buddhist variant, you are more than welcome to use it as well.

For most Qi Gong exercises as well as for everyday life, it is considered beneficial to concentrate on breathing out slowly and deeply. However, since a special depth effect is to be achieved during Embryonic breathing, concentration on inhalation is preferable in this case. In this way, the Qi does not remain in the outer regions of the body (protection Qi), but can easily penetrate deep into the inner meridians, the bone marrow and the Lower Dantian.

There are no time limits regarding the duration of the exercise. In order to achieve an ideal effect, you should aim for an exercise duration of at least 10-15 minutes.

After completing the exercise, you can still place both palms on the lower abdomen for a while and complete the collection and storage of Qi in the Lower Dantian.

Summary of the Embryonic breathing

The Daoist method with a focus on inhalation is generally recommended.

-sitting posture, hands folded in lap, eyes closed
-concentrate on the inhalation (long, conscious inhalation while the exhalation happens by itself)
-reverse abdominal breathing
-on inhalation, imagining that Qi is being breathed through all the pores of the body into the Chong Mai (central channel)
-on the exhale, imagine that Qi is sinking down into the Lower Dantian
-repeat without tension for at least 10-15 minutes
-finally place both hands on the Lower Dantian, return to normal abdominal breathing and long exhalation

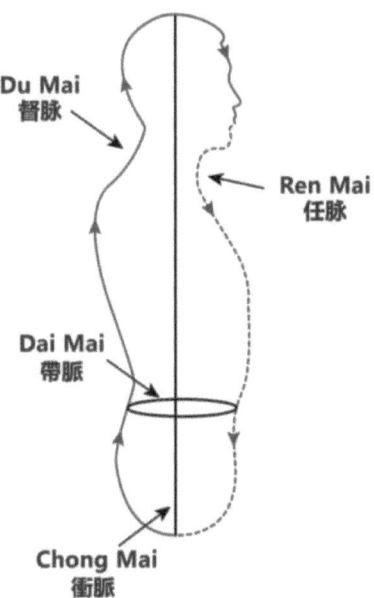

Figure 19

Figure 20

Overview of the practical content of the series

Jin Dao - Stay young with Qi Gong!

Volume 1: The 8 Brocades while standing and the 3 swing exercises

Volume 2: The 18 Tai Chi exercises

Volume 3: The Lohan-Qi Gong

Volume 4: The 8 Brocades while sitting and the small Heavenly circuit

Volume 5: Daoist circle walking and the Game of the 5 animals

Volume 6: Bone Marrow Qi Gong and Embryo Breathing.